Prayer is the Master Key

A

Compilation

By C. D. Dixon

Copyright

Printed in the United States of America.
First Printing, 2016

ISBN-13: 978-098640-033-09

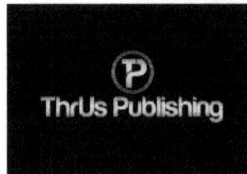

ThrUs Publishing
820 S. MacArthur Blvd #105-166
Coppell, Texas 75019

Dedication

To the body of Christ

Acknowledgments

"For prayer is what we are
more than what we say"

J. Robert Ashcroft.

"Prayer is the key to locking

or unlocking the door"

Matthew 18:18

Also published by

ThrUs Publishing

Get In The Flow: Destiny Is Calling

Compiled By Nell Dixon

Table of Contents

Table of Contents continued

Foreword

Prayer is the most intimate expression of the bride of Christ life. Why, then, is it so neglected?

We live in a time that completely avoids intimacy and closeness. The disposition to avoid self-exposure and friendships I believe affects spiritual as well as interpersonal relationships. The body of Christ, without begin fully aware that this spirit of the age has crept into the church, some believers feel uncomfortable getting too close to God. Prayerlessness is the result.

I believe that part of the body of Christ are more concerned about performing than about being, some refuse to accept the bible reality that human or natural achievement is temporary. But those who understand the work of the Spirit know it is forever eternal. Prayerlessness is really godlessness.

~Apostle CD Dixon

Introduction

Prayer is essential to life. Just as we must breathe and eat to live, we must also pray to survive. There are many ways to make our prayer life effective including writing, being mindful of the words we speak and learning/knowing the Word of God.

Prayer really does work! It is not just a religious ritual, but when entered into sincerely, prayer can bring you closer to God, deliver and protect you from all manners of hurt, harm and danger. There isn't any situation that prayer can't change.

Whether you are suffering from a broken heart, physical afflictions or mental anguish such as un-forgiveness – prayer can deliver you.

Be conscious and deliberate in your decision to pray. Release negative feelings and open your heart to the rewards of prayer: peace, love and understanding.

~Apostle CD Dixon

The

Effectiveness of Prayer

Chapter 1:

Three Keys to Effective Praying

Apostle CD Dixon

One writer says, "God and prayer are inseparable." Notice one thing, out of all creatures that God created; only people pray. I believe that prayer is a gift from God and it keeps the child of God linked to the Father.

There are some things you should be aware of when you pray:

First, remember God does not call you to pray vain prayers, but prayers of faith and praise.

Second, when God calls you to pray for a person expect the answer at any time. Sometimes after years of praying for a person they may seem spiritually unresponsive, but **don't give up!** I repeat **don't give up!**

The Father in Heaven is completing much more than you see right now.

Finally, there is a method to praying effectively…

Key #1: Intercede for Others

Begin focusing only on God.

A. Thank God for the love He has for the person.
B. Thank God for the will of God for the person's life.
C. Thank God for the death, burial and resurrection that Jesus completed for the person.

Offer up praise to God for the person.

True intercessors don't look at the situation, but the revelation. It does not matter how stubborn or difficult the person is, your job as an intercessor is to thank God for the deliverance of the person; while Satan's job is to accuse the brethren. Don't expect God to send the answer to your prayer when your spirit concerning the person is negative.

A. Thank God for the gifts, talents and anointing for the person.
B. Thank God for the good qualities of the person.
C. Thank God for the working of the Holy Ghost in advance for the person although you can't see it with your natural eyes.
D. Thank God for the answer you know is coming in God's timing.

Intercede for the person.

A. Ask God to supernaturally cancel and rearrange Satan's plots against the person.
B. Ask God to bless and reveal his grace and mercy in such ways that the person's spiritual awareness will be heighten to the point that there can be no doubt that it was God's goodness and not coincidence or chance.
C. Ask God to open the heart of the person to obey God's voice, be made aware of personal sin and need for God.
D. Ask God to break all chains of sin, satanic powers or evil habits off and out of the person.

Claim the promise of God for salvation or need.

A. Keep a record of new developing promises that may arise.
B. Ask God for a special promise to manifest for the person.
C. Ask God for a word from the scriptures to hold on to in prayer for the person.

Persevere in prayer.

A. Remind God of your love for the person and remember that God's divine love will never stop reaching out.

B. Keep focus that great prayers don't come instantly. Often it takes time to spiritually remove the person's thinking from error, or willfulness. The person may not be at a place where they can hear the voice of God clearly, so be patient as the Spirit is patient.

C. Every prayer you pray is saved and not lost, maybe the Holy Ghost is speaking in some new way to the person.

D. Understand that the purpose of God manifests first in the mind and heart of the person.

E. Remember that outward actions are often the very opposite of what's happening on the inside of the person.

F. Keep the faith in the face of the enemy when things begin to go wrong.

G. Develop prayer partners to assist you in praying for the person. The test is to unite and not offend.

H. God can tell you what to reveal to the person you are praying for. Even if they show no appreciation at the time, God could bring it back to their remembrance at the time of their deliverance.

Key #2: Agree with other Intercessors

Here are some steps that will allow you, with one or more saints, to follow as your hearts move toward a more complete harmony.

A. Agree that the Father has placed in your heart a need for which to pray.
B. Agree to lay the request before God in the same Spirit and faith.
C. Agree that your deepest drive in prayer is to see the glory of God.
D. Agree that, the petition may be worded different by each intercessor, but the "Amen" will be unanimous.
E. Agree to apply God's promises to the need.
F. Agree in the faith that God will meet the need.
G. Agree that the Father has worked the need out in the Spirit and the Holy Ghost is bringing the answer to pass.
H. Agree to keep pressing in prayer until God answers.
I. Agree to pray together at a certain time, although physically you can't.
J. Agree to submit to God and resist the devil; he will flee from you **(James 4:7)**.
K. Agree that as you hear from God you will bind the enemy regarding the matter **(Matthew 12:19; 18:18-20)**.

L. Agree to give God the glory before and after the answer comes.

Key #3: Know the Benefits of Agreement in Prayer

A. **Agreement in prayer increases the level of awareness of God's presence.** Spiritually we know God is always with us, for God is omnipresent (everywhere at the same time). The saints know that Jesus is always with us when we come together in His name *(Matt. 18:20)*. While interceding with the saints, there is a special anointing that elevates your spiritual awareness of God's presence. Knowing that the Lord hears us when we ask, we have what we ask of Him *(I John 5:15)*.

B. **Agreement in prayer brings clarity to the will of God.** God may reveal His divine will to one of the intercessors in prayer and through that individual to the others. As the believers continue in prayer another person could sense the will of the Father in another aspect of the prayer need. Taking it to another level the Holy Ghost can bring all the intercessors in one accord concerning God's purpose and desire.

C. **Agreement in prayer helps deepen the concern of each intercessor.** Whenever hearts blend in prayer agreement, God takes the depth of a person's desire and deepens the drive and hunger in the other intercessors. You then see the people of God crying in the Spirit or using strong prophetic words which God hears then blesses the whole group. When the intercessors give God true heart hunger, it then gives tremendous power to intercession before God.

D. **Agreement in prayer purifies the prayers.** It is possible while praying not to be there spiritually but having other things on your mind. As many of you continue to pray, God somehow begins to purify, refine, and guide the mind and motives of all who are praying.

E. **Agreement in prayer empowers faith and confidence before the Lord.** The Father is looking for intercessors to pray with deep confidence and holy boldness *(Hebrews. 4:16)*. One may proceed with holy persistence in prayer, while others move with increasing urgency of intercession. This strong confidence is what God is searching for *(Ephesians. 3:12; Hebrews. 10:19)*.

F. **Agreement in prayer increases the level of persistence in prayer.** Those needs in which prayer agreement is necessary tend to be situations in which persistent intercession is essential before God reveals the answer. Jesus had a strong concern that those who followed Him should learn to persist in prayer *(Luke 18:1)*. When the body of Christ agrees in prayer we are an encouragement to each other.

G. **Agreement in prayer delivers spiritual blessing to all intercessors.** When intercessors agree in prayer it deepens the harmony, understanding, and fellowship of the intercessors. It produces the power to strengthen unity in the Spirit *(Ephesians. 4:3, 13)*. I believe disunity is a major hindrance to any intercessor and the effectiveness of prayer.

APOSTLE *Chester D. Dixon* received the call to the gospel ministry at the age of sixteen and began moving in the things of God immediately!

Having exemplified strong leadership qualities at an early age, he became a role model for his peers, and excelled in his academic studies. The Lord birthed a powerful ministry out of Apostle Dixon's spirit called C.D. Dixon Ministries. He attended Prairie View University, majoring in General Business. Apostle Dixon also attended Southwestern Assemblies of God University, where his area of concentration was Pastoral Ministry. While attending (SAGU) Apostle Dixon was also Co-Pastor of God's Love Prayer House Ministries in Dallas Texas founded and Pastored by his mother Beverly J. Baylock-Dixon.

Apostle Dixon is united in holy matrimony with his lovely wife Executive Pastor/Prophetess Nell Dixon and they have three beautiful children. Apostle C.D. Dixon formally Pastored Houston Spiritual Temple World Headquarters. In 1996 the Lord anointed Apostle Dixon as an Apostle. God always anoints before He appoints. Now Apostle Dixon is walking in the appointment of his apostolic calling. In January 2009 "Woodland Spiritual Temple" the second Spiritual Temple was erected by the "Hand of God" through the "Vessel of God"!

Apostle Dixon is the Prophetic Overseer of many conferences and events such as: 40 Days of Fasting & Praying...Couples with A Love Affair...Empowering the Business Mind... Supernatural Encounter...Prophetic Youth Explosion...Spiritual Prophetic Summit and The Gift that Heals. He has conducted revivals, crusades, and conferences in various cities and states. Apostle Dixon has also appeared on several radio stations, internet radio and television programs. God commissioned Apostle Dixon to write a book entitled "An in-depth Study of Prayer" and he is also one of the Featured Authors of Get In The Flow~ Destiny is Calling compilation book. Apostle Dixon is the CEO and Founder of a powerful prayer ministry called Spiritual Kingdom Gate Keepers (SKGK). God has allowed this broken vessel to minister to countless people who have been set free by the power of God's anointing flowing heavily through his preaching and teaching.

With the five-fold ministry at work in his life, and having a heavy apostolic and prophetic mantel, Apostle C.D. Dixon has a contemporary ministry on the "cutting edge" of the millennium. His visionary mandate is to stir up ministry gifts in the body of Christ, equipping men and women for the Kingdom of God, and spiritual warfare. Thus, bringing them to a depth of knowledge, revelation, and maturity in the things of God, so as to effectuate the culmination of the unfinished task of preparing a bride adorned for her husband.

Apostle C.D. Dixon, Sr. Pastor

Twitter @ApostleCDDixon

Facebook @CDDixonministries

Periscope @ApostleCDDixon

Cddixonministries@gmail.com

Instagram @ApostleCDDixon

YouTube @ApostleCDDixon

820 S. MacArthur Blvd. #105-166

Coppell, TX 75019

972-510-5375

Chapter 2
Creating and Maintaining a Prayer Journal

Lady Lavita Crumble

Write the vision, and make it plain upon tables, that he may run that read it. – **Hab. 2:2.**

Keeping a prayer journal is something I have come to realize is vital in this Christian journey. Not only should you write down your prayers, but also the answers to your prayers when they come. If you believe in the prophetic Word of God as well, it is a good practice to write down every prophecy that you receive. It helps to put you in remembrance of the Word of God spoken over your life. I began keeping a prayer journal a few years ago. A very good friend and sister in the Lord shared her journal with me, which gave me insight on how to create my own.

I bought a small journal and began recording my prayers and my daily thoughts. I carried that journal around with me at all times, because I wanted to be prepared when God spoke to me, or when events occurred that were important and memorable. The Lord will give you little nuggets along the way that will help to keep you encouraged. Writing scriptures are also a good idea for your journal. Make sure to date every entry so that when you go back and read through it, you can see where you were spiritually, emotionally and mentally at that particular time in your walk, and how God has spoken to you over the course of your journey. It will also be helpful in seeing how you responded to situations as well.

Keeping a journal is also a way to observe how the hand of God moves chronologically in your life. Consider the journal to be your written petitions to God and His responses to you. You can be open and honest with Him about every aspect of your life. There is nothing you can tell Him that will shock Him. Tell Him exactly how you feel and what you think about your current situation. This written work will be for your eyes only. So write your very deepest thoughts, ideas and imaginations, because the Lord is concerned about everything that concerns you.

"For we have not a high priest which cannot be touched with the feelings of our infirmities…"

- Hebrews 4:15

He will not be offended by what you write. As you mature in the Lord, you will find that your writings will change. So, keeping this journal will also allow you to see your growth.

Using the Word of God in prayer is an excellent way to fortify your prayers. The word will also strengthen you and help build your faith.

"So then faith cometh by hearing and hearing by the Word of God."

– Romans 10:17.

Another benefit to using the Word of God is that the Word is everlasting.

"Heaven and earth shall pass away, but my words shall not pass away."

– Matthew 24:35

Let God's word ring out loud in every situation you are dealing with. You can stand on the accuracy of His word and not your own. When you can't find the words to say, the Word can speak volumes and put you in the right position to pronounce the promises of God over your life and others.

Below are prayers that I wrote in my journal 4 years ago, and the manifestation came in February of 2014 when I met my soon to be husband and on Christmas 2014, when he proposed:

June 8, 2011:

"Father, I thank You that You are mindful of me and You know what I have need of. I bless You for Your grace and mercy towards me."

"I thank You for my husband…a man after Your own heart. A man full of wisdom and compassion. A man of character, strength and integrity. A man who is one with himself and not fragmented by past hurts and disappointments. A man who seeks You daily for direction. A man who orders his day according to Your plans and who walks in tandem step with Your will for his life."

Father, Your word says in **Ecclesiastes 4:9-11**, *Two are better than one; because they have a good reward for their labor. For if they fall, the one will lift up his fellow: but woe to him that is alone when he falleth; for he hath not another to help him up. Again, if two lie together, then they have heat: but how can one be warm alone? Your word also tells us in Genesis 2:18, And the Lord God said, it is not good that the man should be alone; I will make him a help mate for him. So Father You created me to be his companion and I thank You that it shall come to pass, in Jesus' name – Amen."*

June 9, 2011:

"Father, instruct my husband even as he is sleeping **(Psalms 16:7)**, *and in the morning, I pray he will do what's right rather than follow the leading of his own flesh. I know the wisdom of this world is foolishness with You, Lord* **(1 Corinthians 3:19)**. *May my husband not buy into it, but keep his eyes on You and have ears to hear Your voice. A wise man will hear and increase in learning, and a man of understanding will attain wise counsel* **(Proverbs 1:5)**. *Father, teach my husband to seek the counsel of wise Godly men.*

Father, I thank You that my husband and I communicate with one another on the same level. I thank You that we will not argue or allow the sun to go down while we are angry with one another **(Ephesians 4:26)**. *I ask You to help me control my tongue, and help me be careful about what I say* **(Psalms 141:3)**.

I thank You, Father that he and I reason with one another and think before we speak. Father, I thank You that my in-laws and I communicate well and we get along with peace and harmony. There is no division or strife among us. Father I thank You that my husband and I make sound financial decisions."

These prayers were written before I ever met my fiancé. All I can say is that God answered and then some. He is everything that I have prayed for. His parents and I got along great from the very first meeting. As I go back and read through these prayers, I am in awe of God's love, care and attention to detail. He gives us what is necessary and what we want all the time.

I was told that because I wasn't married yet I couldn't pray for my husband, but the Word says in **Romans 4:17b** that we can call those things that be not as though they were.

I stood on the Word until it manifested. Because our words have power to create life or speak death, I can declare and decree a thing and it shall be. I can have whatsoever I say. The same creative speaking power that God has, I know I have because I am one of His children.

As I go back through my journal and read many of the entries, I am encouraged to keep trusting, believing and moving forward.

I am also blessed by God's faithfulness.

MS. *Levita Crumble* is a published author of two books, "Inspirational Reflections," a book of poems and short stories; and "Acts of Betrayal, One Woman's Life Journey to Discovery." Levita is a vocalist, poet, mother of 3 adult children and grandmother of 8. Levita began writing poetry at the age of 16, and developed a love for books as well. She has worked in the legal field for over 20+ years. God has gifted Levita with many talents and abilities. In addition to writing, Levita is also an events coordinator.

For a copy of "Acts of Betrayal", you can purchase a copy on Amazon.com, Barnes & Noble and on iBooks.

Lady Levita Crumble

Twitter - @CrumbleLevita

Facebook - Levita Crumble

LinkedIn - Levita Crumble

Chapter 3
Prayer Must Be a Lifestyle

Pastor Turkeisa Rushin

Greetings my brothers and sisters! I greet you with the full intent to stir up the gift of God in you. Yes! You have a gift from the awesome, loving, kind, and sovereign Lord Almighty on the inside of you. You are one anointed and gifted individual and it is time to come out of hiding and into the full knowledge of who you really are. No longer shall you view yourself as powerless but rather powerful, ineffective but rather effective and impactful. You are unique and it is time to embrace your uniqueness.

Someone, somewhere took the time one day and prayed for you. Now my friend it's time for you to pray for yourself and others with an expectation of timely manifested results, right results. Desire the will of God and God shall do just that, give you His will while at the same time satisfying the desire of your heart which is the will of God. The enemy has tricked people long enough and is being exposed as the deceiver that he really is. Deception is being broken off the minds of the readers of this awesome literary work right now because you are a believer and a seeker. The seeker seeks after the Lord and will surely gain the promise of the Lord which is "The Reward". He is a rewarder to those who diligently seek Him.

Let us pray…

Dear Lord,

I seek you by seeking the Kingdom and I know I am righteous because it came from You to me through my Savior Jesus the Christ. I no longer seek people or flesh but I humbly seek You. I wait patiently on You as I make my petitions and my supplications known unto You. Thank You for adding unto me everything else. I am forever grateful and appreciative for Your grace, mercy, favor, and time. I truly repent for putting anything or anyone before You and Your will. I have turned my heart completely unto You and will worship You in spirit and in truth. This is my prayer of thanksgiving and adoration unto You. I love you eternally and forever long to be in Your presence.

Amen.

Now, don't you feel better? Isn't your mind and heart filled with such love and gratitude unto the Lord now that you have gotten that part out of the way? That is only the beginning. We are in war. The enemy has waged war against all who love the Lord and will stop at nothing because he is angry at God and all who love God. So we must pray and meditate on the Word both night and day. We must never allow it to leave our heart. Confess this prayer along with me as I pray it with and for all the readers of this very passage...

Lord,

Undress us from the things life has dressed us with to cause us to be too heavy to pray effectively and fervently. We behead every giant of opposition right now and shall recover all the spoils stolen from us while we were distracted, in bondage, in error, and even in rebellion and pride. We have come to our senses now and realize that we have had the power and right to recover and be redeemed through Jesus Christ without fail. We employ all of heaven to assist, aid, and complement our recovery and the recovery of all of our loved ones that we are praying for right now. We even include the stranger and the foreigner right now. We accept the faith, power, and endurance for established victory that was already settled for us as we continue witnessing Your great love for us. We are not afraid but have full faith and confidence in You. This is the confidence that we have in You that if we ask anything according to

*Your will that You hear us and if we know that You hear us then we have the petitions, the desires that we ask You (**1 John 5:15**). I believe in the name of the Son of God and I know that I have eternal life according to **1 John 5:13**.*

As I pray, I believe and activate the Word of God for all in prayer because the Word of God is quick and powerful. It's sharper than any double-edged sword. It penetrates even to the dividing of soul and spirit, joints and marrow; it judges the very thoughts and attitudes of the heart according to **Hebrews 4:12***.*

Prayer changes things but it must first change us. We open ourselves up right now for even greater change in us, our hearts, our minds, our spirits, and our souls. We are the product of holy transformation and godly regeneration and it is so in Jesus' Mighty Name, Amen.

I prophesy a greater impact through every reader of this awesome project. You shall reach the unreachable, teach the unteachable, encompass greater longsuffering for the sinner and saint, walk worthy of Kingdom citizenship, do great exploits and emulate Christ in the earth by showing greater love. As **Galatians 5** so eloquently states, "*So I say, live by the Spirit, and you will not gratify the desires of the sinful nature. For the sinful nature desires what* *is contrary to the Spirit, and the Spirit what is contrary to the sinful nature. They are in conflict with each other, so that you do not do what you want."*

To all who are reading this and have sickness in your body and it seems like healing is not making its grand appearance, don't stop believing and claiming your healing. While your here, repent of all sins that you may have committed through thought, word, and/or deed through omission or commission. You still have to repent no matter how long it's been or old it is. Repentance is our daily bread of true conviction. Rid yourself of all un-forgiveness and oughts' against the brethren. You hold too much and release too little. You can get healed from some things by choosing to respond differently, release people, places, and events out of your heart that are keeping you stuck in a moment. Let it GO! Yes, you can and you have to unless you intend on living eternally opposite of heaven. That's right HELL! Hell is for real and you have to make plans to not ever make that your resting place by missing heaven through un-forgiveness and walking in offense.

Free yourself. Choose to accept apologies that

you were never given because if you really think about it, you're probably owing someone a sincere apology yourself but they chose to move on past the situation because they knew how to let dead stuff be dead and live in peace by moving on in their mind and in their spirit. YOU can do that too!!! Pray this prayer with me…

Lord,

I have held on to this thing too long and I'm ready to let this go. I forgive every one that I have held in my heart and I also forgive myself for being my biggest hold up in life, health, and in my relationship with You. I now know that being right is not nearly as important as being righteous and living holy before You. So today I present my body as a living sacrifice, holy, and acceptable unto You my Lord and my King. I will embrace love and Your Love is giving me power right now to even pray for all men. Thank You for Your precious holy ghost. It's making a difference in and through me right now.

The Son has set me free and I am free indeed. Wisdom is mine, knowledge is mine, understanding is mine, faith is mine, joy is mine, peace is mine, and healing is mine. Yes, I am healed from every infirmity and sin of iniquity associated with my hardness of heart and wounded soul. My soul is healed and made whole right now. I am no longer a prisoner to the hard moments of my life and past. My forward progress shall no longer be impeded by self-righteousness and pride. I am washed right now from the old and dressed with the new attire of my new self. Thank You Lord for giving me time and space to get this thing right and to be redeemed from all the time I lost while in darkness(ignorance) of my true freedom.

May the holy fear of God live in me and through me that I may shine the light of His word in the darkness of others who are ready to embrace truth and willing to renounce every way that works against them. I am truly stronger and wiser now! I have truly received and believed the revelation of my healing and my deliverance both spiritually and naturally. I am a testimony! In Jesus' Name I pray, Amen!

As you continue to embrace the life of prayer, your attacks and afflictions may increase but that is all a part of the process of growth. You must know and grow. We cannot stay on milk always and must soon put away the elementary teachings of Jesus Christ.

"Therefore let us leave the elementary teachings about Christ and go on to maturity, not laying again the foundation of repentance from acts that lead to death, and of faith in God, instruction about baptisms, the laying on of hands, the resurrection of the dead and eternal judgement. And God permitting, we will do so. It is impossible for those who have once been enlightened, who have tasted the heavenly gift, who have shared in the Holy Spirit, who have tasted the goodness of the word of God and the powers of the coming age, if they fall away, to be brought back to repentance, because to their loss they are crucifying the Son of God all over again and subjecting him to public disgrace." **(Hebrews 6:1-6)**.

This basically means, some things should not be a problem for us if we really experience Christ and embrace Him and the Word correctly. Then the basics of His teachings will not have to be repeatedly taught to those who have come out of the beginning stages of their relationship and walk with the Lord and grow in the spirit. Yes, promotion and elevation is in the spirit realm as well. It belongs to you and I.

You are victorious and your life, language, mannerisms, character, integrity, and love proves it daily in every situation and circumstance that you face. Now may the grace of God and sweet communion of the Holy Spirit rest, rule, and abide with you His people. May you forever be changed, healed and Holy Ghost filled and baptized into this present day Truth. May every lie be eradicated and every spirit of error be debunked. May you and all connected to you be liberated and acclimated by the True and Living God both now and forever more. You just overthrew everything that once tossed you to and fro. Now give God a praise right there! Prayer is the Master Key! Prayer is a LIFESTYLE!

PASTOR *Turkeisa Vaughn Rushin* is the founding pastor of Empowerment Temple, Inc. located in the small town of Cuthbert, Georgia while residing in Albany, Georgia. She has a well-balanced life as the wife of Delton C. Rushin, mother of Keychard Hill, Keshaun Hill, Khalar Rushin and the step-mother to 2 handsome young men Tyreak Johnson and Kwandarius Rushin. Prophetess Rushin is a nurse by profession and one of the Lord's chosen and sent vessels in this hour to advance the Kingdom and set the captives free through the powerful ministry of the Holy Spirit. She is also an author, entrepreneur, and so many other things to so many people but her life is centered around the call of God on her life and the assignments along with it. Prophetess Rushin loves ministry but loves seeing lives changed and the kingdom of darkness rendered powerless in the lives of all she comes across. Her running anthem is to be a game changer. We are all on the winning team when we are on the Lord's team so it's time to show forth, bring forth, and produce all that we believe the Kingdom is. We are the game changers of today and the leaders to the game changers of tomorrow. We are known by the fruit we bare, produce, and distribute.

Pastor Turkeisa Vaughn Rushin

Facebook. ....Turkeisa Rushin

Twitter.......... rushinwind34

Email........turkeisa1@yahoo.com

Phone. .... (229) 854-9541

The Magnitude of Prayer

Chapter 4
The Four Dimensions
of Intercession

Apostle Marc Richardson

Gen. 2:10-15

10 *And a river went out of Eden to water the garden; and from thence it was parted, and became into four heads.*

11 *The name of the first is Pishon: that is it which compasseth the whole land of Havilah, where there is gold;*

12 *And the gold of that land is good: there is bdellium and the onyx stone.*

13 *And the name of the second river is Gihon: the same is it that compasseth the whole land of Ethiopia.*

14 *And the name of the third river is Hiddekel: that is it which goeth toward the east of Assyria. And the fourth river is Euphrates.*

15 *And the LORD God took the man, and put him into the Garden of Eden to dress it and to keep it.*

It is imperative in this dispensation that the intercessor understands the strategy of God as it pertains to the body of Christ occupying its divine place of dominion. Without a blueprint, pattern, or plan of action the intercessor in this hour will find themselves shooting amiss in the realm of prayer. It is the desire of the enemy for the intercessors of the Kingdom of God to operate from a place of confusion and a place of no order. However, it is the heart of God that we engage the heavens with purpose and power, leaving no room for proposition but total authority when enforcing the mandate of God.

Hidden within the confinement of this scripture we see four strategic places that the intercessors in this dispensation must reign, rule and govern. Without the Government of God reining in authority over these realms we will never bring the earth under divine subjection to the Master and Creator which is God Himself.

The first dimension we see in this text is called "Pishon." Pishon is defined as "increase." Intercessors must pray that the Kingdom of God increase in statue and power, that the Kingdom of God would gain much momentum in the earth to the glory of God. We must not become complacent and satisfied with the souls that are coming in the Kingdom but pursue in the realm of prayer that more would continue to come into the Kingdom. Not only must we increase in souls but we must increase revelation and knowledge of our God. The Bible says that we move from glory to glory, this means that we move from one measure in God to another. There is increase available in the measure of glory **(2Cor. 2:18)** that rest upon His body. Unless the intercessors pray and decree increase, the body of Christ will struggle in its ability to advance in the earth.

The second dimension we see in the text is "Gihon." Gihon is defined as "breakthrough." Being a people of great dominion it is impossible for us to miss the importance of this mantle. Intercessors must continuously exercise our authority to decree breakthrough over the body of Christ. Many in and out of the body are operating under demonic entanglement. This means that unless there is a cry for breakthrough from the intercessor, many souls will never experience the power of God's liberty. The manifestation of a liberated people is the reflection of the King that they serve.

The third dimension that the intercessor must possess is called Tigris. Tigris is defined as the "divine advantage." Satan's goal in the earth is to gain the advantage. The Bible says that we must not remain ignorant to Satan's devices unless he gets the advantage **(2 Cor. 2:11)**. The one with the advantage is the one who operates in dominion. Intercessors must continuously pray that the body of Christ operates from the place of advantage. This can only be done through the power of divine knowledge of the adversary. He who has no respect for his adversary has already lost the battle.

The fourth dimension of the intercessor given in the text is called "Euphrates." This is defined as "fruitfulness." Jesus makes a serious display of a tree that had the ability to bear fruit but never exercised its grace to do so **(Matt. 21:19)**. Would it not be a shame if the body of Christ never maximized the grace granted to us in the earth? To continuously live a life as though we have no power, no influence and no dominion. Intercessors must pray that the body of Christ continues to bear fruit. Fruit is the evidence of dominion and grace. We must pray that we be a body that produces fruit continuously in our works. We must stand out from false and vain worshipers of pagan gods. Our fruit needs to tell the story of our God. The earth is longing for a Kingdom with evidence. The Bible declares in **Romans 8:19** *"For the earnest expectation of the creature waiteth for the manifestation of the sons of God."*

Intercessors must rise up and push the body of Christ to be producers. We must pray that the spirit of bareness be destroyed and buried in this hour.

Prayer Points: In The Name of Jesus

1. I decree that there shall be increase in the body of Christ.
2. I put a demand on every member of the kingdom of God to begin to increase in power, understanding and revelation
3. I decree that there shall be a strong influx of lost souls coming into the Kingdom without delay through the power of the blood of Jesus over their lives.
4. I decree that the people of God will become a people with a lifestyle of breakthrough.
5. I decree there shall be no hindrance of chains and shackles that shall hinder the breakthrough mantle from being active in our lives.
6. I decree full operation from the place of divine advantage.
7. I decree the mantle of wisdom shall fall upon the body with abundance that we will become fully knowledgeable of the devices of the enemy.
8. I decree that we shall have the advantage in the marketplace. That the systems of men will

come under the subjection of the dominion of our God.

9. I decree that we shall never be a barren people.

10.I decree that we shall be abundant fruit producers with divine manifestation of the Kingdom that we occupy and represent.

APOSTLE *Marc Richardson* is an insightful, passionate, provocative, prolific speaker and teacher who serves as the Founder and Overseer of Kingdom City Global Ministries.

Apostle Marc's ministry reaches beyond the nations and color barriers whose purpose is to gather and build a massive army of warriors that will yield themselves to the Father in order to forcefully advance the Kingdom of God in the earth.

As a man after the heart of God, this powerful, anointed visionary flows in the Apostolic Dimension, setting Kingdom Order and foundational stability among the Body of Christ. His heavenly mandate and assignment is to execute and flow in the six-fold mantle according to **Jeremiah 1:10**; *"Behold I set thee over nations and kingdoms, to root out and to pull down, to destroy and to throw down, to build and to plant"*. His indelible mark is reclaiming territories for the Kingdom, provoking and loosing healing and deliverance, building, establishing and equipping people in preparation for the return of Christ Jesus our

Lord. Walking in this mantle, lives are changed and empowered, gifts activated and sons and daughters are flowing in their God ordained call.

Apostle Marc was saved and filled with the Holy Ghost at the age of 9 years old at Antioch Baptist Church in Hampton, Virginia, where his late uncle, Howard V. Booker was his Pastor and spiritual mentor for many years. He is the younger of two siblings born in Hampton, Virginia to James and the late Estella Richardson. He is the father of three children Zion, Jordan and Kamryn.

Apostle L.M. Richardson

Kingdom City Global Ministries
240-743-0379
9504 Calvert Manor Ct.
Ft. Washington, MD. 20744

Chapter 5
Prayer Really Works!

Prophetess Arma Fuller

Praise God for this opportunity to share my testimonies and experiences on how prayer worked for me. My experiences with prayer have been marvelous. I've learned when praying you must pray without doubting and wavering but in faith. *Now faith is the substance of things hoped for, the evidence of things not seen.* **(Hebrews 11:1)**

I was reminded of how prayer worked for me when the enemy tried to get my son through smoking drugs. At first I couldn't believe what was actually happening. Later on after thinking about it I immediately realized this was the work of the enemy. I said, "Devil you won't have my child he is my seed and I am a child of the Most High God." As a mother I tried to fix it by myself but my way didn't work. The scripture tells us to *"Trust in the Lord with all thine heart, and lean not unto thine own understanding. In all thy ways acknowledge him and he shall direct thy path."* At that moment is when I said okay God I trust you to protect and deliver him. **(Proverbs 3:5-6)**

At that time, I started praying for the spirit of obedience to be stirred up in me so I would obey God no matter what occurred concerning my son. The Holy Spirit gave me two promises on obedience. *Behold, to obey is better than sacrifice, and to hearken than the fat of rams.* **(1Samuel 15:22b)** I realized I had to totally trust God to keep me at peace through the delivering process. If ye be willing and obedient, ye shall eat the good of the land.

Finally, I began to see just how important my obedience was to God. I knew then that everything was going to be fine and that my son would be delivered

As I began to seek God concerning the problem he began to speak and reveal to me what to pray about. First God told me to pray without ceasing. He said this deliverance requires some pressing, fasting and praying too. Pray without stopping even when it looks like things are getting better. *"Pray without ceasing."* **(1Thessalonians 5:17)** *And he said unto them, this kind can come forth by nothing, but by prayer and fasting.* **(Mark 9:29)** This was a stubborn demon but I had the Word in my mouth to kill that demon at the root. God started to awaken me throughout the night to pray and I would get up regardless of how I felt at that time. Many times I would call my prayer partners to agree with me in prayer. Sometimes God would even tell me to sow a seed to a certain ministry and I would because I was determined that the enemy would not have my child. My son's deliverance was connected somewhat to me obeying God's instruction.

Several times God gave me this scripture, **Luke 22:31-32** *"And the Lord said, Simon, Simon, behold Satan hath desired to have you, that he may sift you as wheat: But I have prayed for thee, that thy faith fail not; and when thou art converted, strengthen thy brethren"*. I stood on this scripture when the enemy tried to attack him the most. I would pray and quote this scripture and serve notice on the enemy that he could not have my child because he belongs to God.

One time my son had an accident and his car flipped over twice. The enemy was defeated again because he did not suffer from one broken bone, no scratches or bruises on him or his ex-wife anywhere! During the time of the accident, God woke me up telling me to pray now and I obeyed. Look at how God will move when you pray! God protected him from the enemy's trap because of the prayers of the righteous and my obedience. *The effectual fervent prayers of a righteous man availeth much.*

If you stand in faith when you pray God will answer and will be right on time. **(James 5:16b)**

Once the store clerk pulled a gun on him and the gun jammed. Look at God move again! The prayers of the righteous *availeth* much. Prayers of the righteous will confuse the enemy and make him back up and go in another direction.

There were times when my son would run out of gas and even have flats on the freeway in the wee hours of the morning. God would still protect him from seen and unseen danger.

There were times when it seemed like my son was getting worse instead of better. I believed God would do what he said, save and deliver my child. My son starting loosing good jobs, couldn't pay bills on time, his car was always breaking down, and he couldn't keep money and even dropped out of school.

I kept praying and speaking the Word of God over the situation. **(Isaiah 59:19b)** *"When the enemy shall come in like a flood, the Spirit of the Lord shall lift up a standard against him.* I would pray and command the enemy to let him go in Jesus' name. I would cancel the contract of the enemy on my son's life and plead and cover my son under the blood of Jesus. After totally giving my son over to God I began to see changes happening in his life. I never fussed or beat him over the head. I would just pray and tell him, "Son God is going to deliver and bring you out." I would decree the Word over him that he was free and whom the Son set free is free indeed. **(John 8:36)** *If the son therefore shall make you free, ye shall be free indeed.*

My mind was made up that no weapon formed against my son would prosper. **(Isaiah 54:17)** *"No weapon that is formed against thee shall prosper; and every tongue that shall rise against thee in judgment thou shall condemn. This is the heritage of the servants of the Lord, and their righteousness is of me"* said the Lord.

My son's deliverance didn't come over night or as soon as I would have liked it to. The deliverance process took five years but I kept praying, believing, and standing on the word of God. My faith was tried and tested many times during this process. At times my prayer life got weak but I fought hard to stay strong and not let the enemy win. I knew that I loved God and so did my son even though my son was smoking he would kneel and pray every time he got ready to step out the door. I knew that, *"All things work together for good to them that loved God, to them who are called according to his purpose."* **(Romans 8:28)** God was still extending His grace on my son. We must never quit praying for our children no matter how big the problem looks because God will answer your prayers. God is faithful and just. He will deliver and bring them out.

One day after five years my son came to my home. He sat on the stairs in my home said, *"Mama I am tired of smoking. I want a better life for me. I laid on my face last night and prayed to God to take the taste of smoking out of my mouth and away from me."* I was so happy and excited about what God had done in him.

I am pleased to tell you today he is delivered completely from smoking. My son is married now four years to a beautiful lady and the father of two beautiful daughters. He is a hardworking man, great father, super husband, awesome son and man of faith.

Yes! Look at God! He answered the prayer of the righteous. Hallelujah!

Prayer is the key to your problem and faith unlocks the doors. Prayer is everything to me simply because I know that God will answer your prayers when you pray in faith. You can tell every mountain to be removed because you know that God will move on your behalf.

PROPHETESS *Arma Nell Fuller* has been called and chosen by God. She is a woman of faith and operates under the anointing of the Holy Spirit.

Prophetess Fuller is a native of Gloster, Louisiana. She was born February 16, 1960. She was educated in the public school system in Gloster, Louisiana and Houston, Texas. She moved to Houston, Texas in 1975 and still resides there now. She is an only child with the heart of God, the mind of Christ, and the Spirit of God. She has been married for 9 years, blessed with five lovely children, three sons and two daughters, is also blessed with three lovely daughter-n-laws and eight gorgeous grandchildren.

Prophetess Fuller accepted Christ as her personal Lord and Savior at an early age, realized that she was unique and had a calling on her life. She accepted her calling to preach the Gospel of Christ to a dying world on February 3, 1993. She has faithfully served the Lord through His work in many areas of the church including, but not limited to Sunday school teacher, Sunday school secretary, President of the Senior Usher Department,

President of the Women's Mission Department, President of the Intercessory Team, and altar worker. She is a member of Spiritual Temple of Dallas where the overseers are Apostle C.D. Dixon and Prophetess Nell Dixon.

Prophetess Fuller is an ordained minister, prayer warrior, intercessor, mother and founder of Kingdom Builder's Homeless Ministry and Kingdom Builder's Anointed Prayer Ministry. This ministry has a twenty-four hour prayer request website as well as a prayer line where she and fellow prayer warriors intercede day and night on behalf of others. This ministry was birthed on January 1, 2000 in Shreveport, Louisiana with two members, Prophetess Fuller and Sister Eddie Marie Pickney and now it has grown immensely thanks to the grace of God.

Prophetess Fuller walks in the office of her calling and she embraced her calling as she embraces her calling as a Prophetess. She was ordained on September 23, 2011.

Prophetess Fuller has the Heart of God and is fueled by the passion for God's people through preaching the uncompromising Word of God, praying, prophesying, encouraging, edifying, and exhorting. She is a servant and a willing vessel of God. She believes in the Five-Fold Ministry and she believes that the anointing of the Holy Spirit removes burdens and destroys yokes.

Prophetess Arma Nell Fuller-Cole

3838 Gamlin Bend Drive
Houston, TX 77082
832-607-1905

Facebook- Arma Nell Fuller-Cole
Twitter- @ArmaFuller
Instagram-@ArmaFuller
Email- armafuller@gmail.com &
armafuller@att.net

Chapter 6

Protection & Deliverance From Death

through Witchcraft (A Prayer)

Minister Linda Cole

Father God,

In Jesus' name I come into your presence with a heart of thanksgiving. Thanking You for Your word in **Psalms 23:4-6** which says that,

"Yea thou I walk through the valley of the shadows of death, I will fear no evil for thou art with me. Thou rod and thou staff they comfort me. Thou prepare a table before me in the presence of my enemy, Thou anointed my head with oil my cup runneth over. Surely goodness and mercy shall follow me all the days of my life and I shall dwell in the house of the Lord forever," Amen.

Father, I pray in Jesus' name for all who are under the influence and attack of witchcraft. I ask that you would shield their mind just as you shielded mine from all demonic dreams, demonic visions, hijacking of thoughts, confusion, hearing voices and all other attacks of the mind. Let the Blood of Jesus be upon the gate to their minds. Father Your word says in **Isaiah 26:3** that, "Thou wilt keep him in perfect peace, whose mind is stayed on thee: because he trusteth in thee." You also said in **Proverbs 3:5** to, "Trust in the Lord with all thy heart and lean not onto thy own understanding but in all thy ways acknowledge Him and He shall direct thy path."

Holy Spirit, help them as you have helped me by guarding their mind and enabling them to keep their mind stayed on Jesus in spite of what is going on in their head. Give them peace in their mind and in their heart in the midst of the storm. Help them to not become fearful because of what they are going through or what they see in the spirit realm. Cover them and their dwelling place under the Blood of Jesus.

*Let **Psalms 91** become a reality to them as it is to me. When demons or human spirits come to torment them, send your warring angels from heaven to war on their behalf just as you sent them to war for me during my encounter with human spirits and demons that showed up in my home whenever they felt like it to attack me.*

*Put an end to their trespassing by cutting their lay lines in the name of Jesus. Let it be unto them according to Your word in **Psalms 35:6** Let their way be dark and slippery and let the angel of the Lord persecute them. Father, deliver them from their fears according to **2 Timothy 2:7** "For God hath not given us the spirit of fear; but of power, and of love, and of a sound mind." You said in your word, **Psalms 27:1, 2** "The LORD is my light and my salvation; whom shall I fear? The LORD is the strength of my life; of whom shall I be afraid? When evildoers came upon me to devour my flesh, my* *adversaries and my enemies, they stumbled and fell."*

Help them Holy Spirit to stand on the Word of God by getting it into their spirit so that they can walk in it.

Heavenly Father, guard their souls just as you have guarded mine from the soul hunters of the night. Let their souls escape from the soul hunters that come to surround their souls at night to imprison them. Let it be unto them as your word says in **Psalms 124:7** *"Our soul has escaped as a bird from the snare of the fowlers the snare is broken, and we have escaped."*

Thank You Jesus for being the anchor of our souls according to Hebrews 6:19 This hope [this confident assurance] we have as an anchor of the soul [it cannot slip and it cannot break down under whatever pressure bears upon it] – a safe and steadfast hope that enters within the veil [of the heavenly temple, that most Holy Place in which the very presence of God dwells], Hallelujah.

Father, I pray in Jesus' name that You would meet each and every need of your people according to Your Word in **Philippians 4:19** *"But my God shall supply all your needs according to His riches in Glory by Christ Jesus."*

Provide for them Father as You provided for me when the enemy attacked my finances by sending rivers of drought into my life to the point that I lost everything and was instructed by You to move into a shelter for refuge.

Every day You met each and every need that I had. Just as Your Word says in **Psalms 37:25** "I have been young, and now am old; yet have I not seen the righteous forsaken, nor his seed begging for bread." Let Your Word become a reality to Your people Father as they continue to trust in You.

Father, Your Word says in **Isaiah 53:5**, "But he was wounded for our transgressions, he was bruised for our iniquities: the chastisement of our peace was upon him; and with his stripes we are healed." I pray for those whose bodies have become plagued with all types of sickness and disease from the attacks of witchcraft. Those whom the enemy has left feeling defeated, feeling as if they can't go on. I ask that you would deliver them from such attacks as you have delivered me during my darkest hour. The hour when the enemy hit me with his final blow, leaving me for dead lying flat on my back. The hour when I was unable to speak, unable to breathe, in and out of conscience, unable to pray, seeing people walk around my bed and as I reached out to touch them they weren't there. This is the hour that all I could do was to keep my mind on Jesus and constantly cry out for mercy.

I pray that Your people would call out to You asking that You would have mercy on them as I did according to Your Word in **Lamentations 3:22, 23** It is of the LORD'S mercies that we are not consumed, because his compassions fail not. They are new every morning: great is thy faithfulness. Hallelujah!

Father, I pray Your Word in **Romans 8:11** over Your people, "But if the Spirit of him that raised up Jesus from the dead dwelleth in you, he that raised up Christ Jesus from the dead shall give life also to your mortal bodies through his Spirit that dwelleth in you."

I pray that You would resurrect every dead thing that the enemy has killed within Your people just as You have resurrected me from the clutches of death. For **Psalms 138:7** says "Though I walk in the midst of trouble, You will revive me; You will stretch forth Your hand against the wrath of my enemies, And Your right hand will save me." I pray that You would revive them according to Your Word just as You have revived me and delivered me out of my troubles. I pray that You would send a revival into their spirits.

Remember God's word says in **1 Corinthians 15:57,** *"But thanks be to God, which giveth us the victory through our Lord Jesus Christ,"* **2 Corinthians 2:14** *"Now thanks be unto God, who always causeth us to triumph in Christ and who maketh manifest through us the savor of His knowledge in every place."*

So Father we decree and declare the victory over all witchcraft attacks in Jesus' name we pray,

Amen.

MINISTER *Linda Cole* was called into the ministry at an early age. She attended bible school at Eagles Nest Church in the early 90's where she also received ordination into the ministry. She spent over 5 years ministering in several prisons thru out the State of Texas to teens, men and women under the ministry of Bishop T.D. Jakes.

She received a certificate for serving in this Ministry as well as several Lay Counselor Certificates. One thru Lighthouse University and the other thru Trinity Cross Ministries. She has volunteered with several homeless shelters throughout the Dallas Fort Worth Metroplex working with broken, hurting, displaced people.

She received a certificate during her stay at Dallas Life Foundation after completing a 10-month program which has enabled her to go back into the shelter to mentor women. She loves being a servant for God and has a God given passion to work with the broken, hurting, displaced people of today to help them find their way to Christ.

Minister Linda Cole

Email: colelinda50@gmail.com

Facebook: Linda Cole

LinkedIn: Linda Cole

Chapter 7

My Life ... Influenced by the power of prayer!

Prophetess Martha Blanding

Through prayer, I have seen the hand of God in my life even up to the point where I received Christ. I look back, even at my childhood! Born as a twin to a mother who faced circumstances of having to give her newborn twins away at birth and watching them being placed in foster care, put up for adoption, signing the papers, and not knowing where or with whom they would be placed. I know it was her prayers that God heard in order for this wonderful couple to be placed in a situation where they couldn't have children. My parents desired a boy, but chose to adopt my sister and myself together!

Our parents loved and cared for us, we attended church faithfully, and learned about God through our parents through the lives they lived. They both were deeply enthralled in the community, church and business. As an adult, I found myself knowing about church but, not really knowing who God really was. I knew what it meant to be Baptist but, not what it meant to have a relationship with Christ. I remember hearing my father praying every Sunday. Daddy would get on his knees and pray these long melodious prayers.

I remember saying to myself "I wonder who he is talking too?" As a child I saw God as a being "somewhere out there". I couldn't grasp the connection between what it meant to "Pray to God."

Upon graduating High School, I spent the next 6 years in the United States Air Force and another 4 years in nursing school. During that time, I continued to attend church, but I ventured out and decided to learn about other religions thru my studies and attending other denominational services.

I found myself yearning to know and to communicate with the "God of Martha" and not her father. I prayed and asked God to show me who He was and to let me know He was there. I finally received Christ at the age of 28. I was led to Him by this wonderful minister Jettie Davis in Montgomery, Alabama. Jettie would hang out with me after network marketing events, pray for me and with me while traveling to give presentations.

I remember always bringing a CD of gospel music that she would always politely ask, "Do you mind if we listen to this?" I remember a group of us (including Jettie) deciding what our plans would be for New Year's Eve. My tradition was to go to the club with my friends but, Jettie made the suggestion that we go to church. I remember church being different that night. I remember praying the Sinners Prayer with Jettie and that night I received Christ. From that night forward, my Life was never the same. He heard my prayers!!!

As a result of prayer and seeing Christ as my personal Savior, I continued to pray and ask God to show me His ways because I so desired to see God in a loving way. The only side of God I knew about was the God of Hell Fire and brimstone! The Lord led me to study the ways of a "healthy father". I studied the word of God as well as listen to series on Healthy Fathers and how He acted and communicated. It helped me to relate to God in a softer way and actually brought me closer to HIM. I saw HIM as a God of Grace, love, compassion, mercy and kindness. One I never knew.

Throughout the rest of my 20's and 30's I continued in prayer and was lead into an unrelenting passion for Christ. His ways, His people and what it meant to "walk out my destiny". In 2000 I embarked upon obtaining a fashion degree from The Fashion Institute of Technology in New York and a second degree from The Fashion Institute of Design and

Merchandising in Los Angeles, California. All the while I continued to stay connected to my faith. I have found that before every move to a different city I would always ask God to lead me to the right place. HE would always tell me in a dream or vision where to go next.

I see prayer as a navigation tool. In the military, we used a compass as our guide. I had no clue how to use a compass, but the leader of the platoon knew how to use it and instructed the rest of us. I see God as being the expert and prayer being the "compass".

We must communicate with God and He downloads our instructions through prayer (compass) in order to direct us. Without prayer, we run the risk of being led into places, people, and even marrying people who were not God-sent. The danger of prayerlessness is that it may take a minute to get into a situation, but years to get out and be delivered. Even as a nurse, working with psychiatric patients, I've seen the effects of a person being bound by addictions and habits that have gripped them and have had a lifetime hold that robs them of a "free life."

In my own life I've noticed times of being afflicted by ghosts of the past (abandonment, rejection, fear, anxiety etc.) that seemed to interfere with my prayer life and living a life of "freedom." In those times, I found myself praying and God would send immediate help. Case in point, 5 years ago I was going through a struggle and asked God to help me. One day I was leaving my home and casually spoke to my new neighbor. As time went on, we always seemed to cross paths and share light conversations. One day I decided to attend a new church in my community and guess who just happened to be sitting 1 pew over? My Neighbor! Upon my next encounter, I found out she was a Christian counselor! Just what the doctor ordered! I wasted no time enrolling and didn't care what it cost!

Through prayer, I knew this process would be brief and I needed to fully subscribe, start, take it seriously, participate and finish. Nine weeks later she announced she was moving her practice to Florida! That was just enough time for me to go through the process and change the course of my life.

One week later I was invited by a friend to join a prayer line. At that time, I had no clue what a prayer line was or why I needed to participate. I noticed everyone was given the opportunity to pray. I remember saying please don't call on me! I was paralyzed with fear! I remember hearing the Leader of the prayer line, Prophetess Arma Nell Fuller-Cole, praying and it floored me that this lady could pray for hours on end! I said God, is she reading from a book? How did she memorize all that! Lol! Needless to say, I stuck with it, soaked it up like a sponge, came to love prayer and actually began to tag team with her in praying for God's people.

We would witness people being healed, prayers being answered and the Word of the Lord being revealed through prophecy. Needless to say, to this very day, I have found that prayer and praying for others, gives me such a sense of service and accomplishment. Seeing how the hand of God has been covering me throughout my life and others is breathtaking! I can't wait to see what is next!

PROPHETESS ELECT *Martha Blanding*

is a native of South Carolina and a graduate of T.L. Hanna High School. Upon completing high school, she entered the USAF as a medic. Shortly thereafter, she graduated from Troy State school of Nursing with a Bachelor's of Science in Nursing. Desiring to follow her life-long dream to become a fashion designer, she was accepted in 2001 to the Fashion Institute of Technology in New York City where she became a fashion designer with a specialization in tailoring. She was a design intern in two major fashion businesses located in The Garment District in New York City. She was also an assistant to George Simonton who is a women's fashion designer and has a great following and appears regularly on QVC.

In 2006, she graduated from the Fashion Institute of Design and Merchandising in Los Angeles, California with a Degree in Apparel Manufacturing Management where she studied the Business of Fashion.

Prophetess Blanding accepted her call into the ministry in 1994 where she served under the ministry of Bishop George D. Lee III at the

Cathedral of the Holy Spirit in Augusta, Georgia.

During this time, she learned and served in the Apostolic and Prophetic ministry. She was also co-anchor of their weekly video presentations and television ministry.
She was ordained as a Prophetess in 2011 Kingdom Covenant Fellowship of Churches and furthered her Training in 2012 in the school of the Prophets at Zion Ministries in Bedford Texas with Apostle Mickey and Prophetess Sandie Freed.

Prophetess Blanding is also the owner and designer of *Custom Robes and Designs by Martha.* She designs custom ministerial garments, choir robes, praise dance and theatrical garments. She is also a custom cake artist and owns a business creating custom specialty cakes including wedding cakes! The name of the business is *Custom Cakes & Design by Martha.*

She has three siblings: Mary, Tracey and James, has 17 nieces and nephews and owns an awesome Dog named Cooper.

Prophetess Martha Blanding

The Power of Prayer

Chapter 8

Prayer Changes Situations

Ms. Jacqueline McDaniel

My Mother introduced my sisters, brothers, and I to Christ at an early age. My mother knew that one day we would come into the full knowledge of who God was, and that we would all be saved. By the time I was 8 years of age, I was singing in the choir, participating in Christmas plays, doing Easter speeches, and participating in Sunday school as well. However, I still didn't know who God was. I only knew that He existed and that He created the heaven and the Earth.

It reminds me of a scripture in **Acts 17:23**. [23] *for as I passed by, and beheld your devotions, I found an altar with this inscription, TO THE UNKNOWN GOD. Whom therefore ye ignorantly worship, Him declare I unto you.*

That was me! I really didn't know who God was, I just did a lot of participating in church. Sometimes we become ignorant of who He is and little did I know, that was about to change. I was going to know that God was a living, loving, graceful, faithful, forgiving, and full of mercy God.

It was in the month of September and I remember sitting in my class room, when all of a sudden I felt like God was calling me home.

As I pondered this feeling, I could not shake it off. So when I got home I thought about telling my mother about it, but I didn't. The reason I didn't was because I knew that the only person that could help me was God the Almighty. That night, I lay in my bed and prayed to God to not to take me yet, and to let me live to see another day. When morning came I was grateful that he allowed me to wake up so as I got ready for school I didn't think about it much, because I knew God had answered my prayer and that it was over. At the end of school that day, I felt the same way again but this time it was much stronger and I knew that God had not answered my prayer. I sat there in the class room and didn't want to go home. I dreaded going to bed at night and the only thing I knew to do was to pray, just pray. I kept telling myself that God will hear my prayer.

This went on for a period of 2 weeks and I felt like God's answer to me would be NO!! Death had become frightening and fearful to me because I didn't understand it. So each night I prayed and asked the Lord to forgive me of my sins, to wait until I got married, have kids, and to see my grandkids. I also remember being very fearful of even falling asleep or closing my eyes.

As I would lay in my bed I WANTED God to not hide his face from me in the day when I needed him the most. According to **Psalms 102**, *Hide not thy face from me in the day when I am in trouble; incline thine ear unto me: in the day when I call answer me speedily.*

I wanted God to incline his ear unto me in the day when I call. I wanted God to answer me speedily. I needed a right now answer, but as I prayed my prayers every night I noticed my prayers began to become longer and sincere. At the end of my prayer I asked God to show me a sign that he had heard my prayer and that he would permit me to live. Each night I prayed faithfully to God never giving up, keeping faith that he will lengthen my days here on earth. I am reminded of Hezekiah and how God answered his prayer and extended his life.

According **Isaiah 38:2**, *Then Hezekiah turned his face to the wall and prayed to the LORD, and said, "Remember now, O LORD, I beseech You, how I have walked before You in truth and with a whole heart, and have done what is good in Your sight." And Hezekiah wept bitterly.*

So as I was sitting in my classroom, a multitude of lights began to shine all around my body. At first I was shocked, because I didn't know what it was. So as I looked with amazement, I knew that God had answered my prayer. I KNEW I had an experience with Him, I would find Him to be faithful to His word, and He heard me from His holy hill. This happened, on a Friday at noon and unto this day I still see the multitude of lights.

I know that God kept His promise to an 8-year-old girl who didn't know what prayer really was or who God was until she called upon Him and found Him to be faithful and full of love. So if you would seek Him with a pure heart and have faith, He will answer you. Because we as Christian's represent Christ in Word and Deed and we will be judged on everything we SAY and DO.

As I think back during that time I knew God was only preparing me, molding me and shaping me, while showing me who He was. Now in my times of desperation, stress and when I am perplexed or confused about something, I get on my face and pray to God because I know He holds the answer to all my questions. If I don't get an answer right away,

I just wait. You have to pray with a pure heart, clean hands, humble yourself and have faith that God will hear you as well. Prayer is a process. It's more than just saying a lot of eloquent words. Your heart has to be pure because good and evil can't come from the same heart. From this experience I praise God for this testimony and for letting me get to know Him. I AM SO GRATEFUL!

MS. *Jacqueline McDaniel* was born to the parents of Willie Mae Harper and Walter Harper of Tyler, Texas.

Jacqueline has 4 Children, 3 Boys and 1 Daughter, who she is very proud of.

Ms. McDaniel's mother served as a licensed missionary and also sang in the choir as well. Her father was head of the Deacon Board and sang in the choir as well. Jacqueline was also the youth Sunday school teacher and she was the youth choir director. She feels that our youth should be equipped with the Word of God and knowing who God is, especially with so many different religions that exist in the world today. She was a member of the praise and worship team.

When she moved to Dallas, Texas, she knew the voice of God was calling her into a deeper relationship with Him. She was also a Graduate of Hannah's Sons and Daughters Intercessory Prayer school and Rabbi Josue School of Intercessory Prayer as well.

She believes that having a prayer life is an effective way of communicating with God, you have to have the love of God and the love for others for your prayer to become effective. Love is not something that you can pick up and put back down. We must be able to love unconditionally.

Ms. Jacqueline McDaniel

1640 Knight Trail, Frisco, TX 75034

(214) 799-675

Chapter 9
God Will Mend
Your Broken Heart

Evangelist Cynthia McKnight

Psalm 147:3 *He heals the broken hearted and binds up there wounds*

April 25th 2013, 4:30pm, I received a phone call that my oldest son, Rayvon had been shot and I needed to get to Thirteenth Street right away. I informed my husband, Jeanarol, that our son had been shot. He was driving so fast I had to tell him to slow down and to remain calm. As he drove, I prayed in my mind and convinced myself Rayvon was ok. Boy was I wrong! When we got to the scene, all I saw was yellow tape everywhere. It was then that I knew my first born son was gone.

Anxiety set in. I could not breathe. I looked to my right and saw a sister from a former church and asked her to pray for me. After she prayed, I was a little calm but needed to sit down. They put me in our truck and I just cried so hard. It was a deep cry, something that I had never experienced before. All of a sudden, I got angry. Not at God, but at the devil and vowed I would snatch more souls from the fire than the one son he took from me. As I looked around my family was in shock and I didn't know what to do for them. Honestly, I didn't know what to do for myself. I called my church, World Outreach and Bible Training

Center and they showed up. Its seemed like my whole church was there laying hands and praying for people the site blew my mind. As I watched God use his people to pray for my family and friends I was so taken back. People got prayer who may have never gotten it if Rayvon was with us. Genesis 50:20 was taking form in my life right before my very eyes.

It was very late when we got home and there are no words for the many things that were going through my mind. As I sat on the side of the bed watching my husband sleep, something was happening. All of a sudden the ugliest feeling I had ever felt tried to take hold of me. Immediately I cried out to the Lord saying. "Lord I need you! No-no, please help me! Lord I can do this, but only if you help me. I can't do it alone, but if you help me I can make it." And immediately as quick as that demon came, it left.

I woke up that morning knowing that there was so much to be done, but thanks be unto God who knows all things Rayvon's father handled everything. This was a blessing because I am married and he was engaged to someone and there was no time for strife. In the mist of all that was going on I had ministry to run Chat&Chew Real Women Real Talk. I was thinking of canceling but a close family friend said I shouldn't so I took her advice. The day of the group over forty women came out to support me and women were saved, healed and delivered and I was encouraged.

The following day, I had to go and find an outfit. I took my daughter with me. The process was overwhelming and I started to have an anxiety attack and needed to sit down. Haly got me a chair and informed the sales person, that she knew was saved, about what had happened so she and about three other women surrounded me and began to pray. My God it was powerful! It was one lady who stood out because she had informed me that she lost her son in a fire a few years back. To my surprise I found out she was the wife of a known pastor in the city of Milwaukee, Wisconsin. All I could say was wow! **Genesis 50:20**, was not taking form, but took form in my life and I knew it. I really was not in the mood for a candle light vigil but my family really wanted to so I finally said yes. We informed everyone as well as the TV Stations. My Church family came out to support me and God showed up at that place there were over two hundred people at that vigil. Now the most powerful thing that happened once again people were receiving prayer and getting hands laid on them. God was getting the glory at every turn.

God was making sure I was being taking care of every step of the way. A couple of days before Rayvon's home going I received a phone call from Rayvon's pastor he wanted to talk with me. This is what he said. On Sunday Rayvon was the first in line at the altar for prayer. The Holy Spirit said I want you to pray for him last and when you pray for him I want you and the elders to surround him. We did as the Lord said and the power of God fell. He told me my son loved the Lord and was one of his best members. He also told me that Rayvon was going to be a deacon and receive his new members' papers. They wanted me to come to a service in honor of Rayvon on that next Sunday. The Lord was assuring me that Rayvon was with him and wanted me to be confident of the promise he made to me.

When I was a young saved woman at the age of 25 on my knees praying, the Lord told me he was going to save all five of my children. **Genesis 50:20**. The day of Rayvon's home going was here and God had put strength on me that not only blew my mind but the people around me. We had Rayvon's home going at a very big church in Milwaukee, WI. I was amazed when I walked in that church it was full wall to wall people were standing room only, all in the balcony, my God people were everywhere. I could not believe all the people that were there. It was definitely a sight to see.

As the service was going on in the mist of all those people, I just began to give God praise for all he had done. I was so grateful for the twenty-six years I had gotten with Rayvon. Rayvon was an extraordinary human being who loved his daughter and his family and friends, but most of all he loved the Lord. He was on his way somewhere in the Lord. The following day I was just resting and received a phone call that the two young men who had murdered my son were in custody and being booked. We were to meet them at Rayvon's father's house for all the details. I had made up my mind before I even knew who had killed my son that I would forgive them and hearing the details of what happened would not change that for me. I was not going to give the enemy any room at all to use this thing to destroy my life.

As the days ahead came I began to get many inboxes on social media from different people asking me to pray for them. I was in shock because I thought I was the one who needed prayer but they saw something that I didn't see, the strength of God. It was as if God Himself stood up on the inside of me. I now can identify with one of my favorite stories Footprints in the Sand. Yes I was and am being carried right up to this very day. It has been three years since Rayvon went home to be with the Lord and God is mending my broken heart every day. I was one told by a church mother to have whatever emotion I needed to have but never stay there. This advice has helped me up until this very day. I believe that the prayer I prayed on Thursday April 25th 2013 changed my whole life. Yes, it could have went the other way but I love the Lord too much and I know he loves me and he has shown me that my whole life.

I really see **Philippians 4:7** *The peace of God which surpasses all understanding will guard your hearts and minds in Christ Jesus.* The Lord had done all this for me and more. I pray every day to be ok for God to keep me in a good place. I have set out on a mission, helping other mothers to find the peace and strength that

God has so mercifully given to me. I want them to know that this same peace and strength is readily available to them if they yield to it. God understands, He will always understand. Even though Jesus was not taken but given for us.

God still went through seeing His son suffer for mankind. God knows what it's like to lose a child. But He knows the joy of getting him back. We will get our children back when we make it to heaven. Yes, we will see them again. I hope that my story helped you in some way. Prayer was and is The Master Key for My Life.

EVANGELIST *Cynthia McKnight* is the Founder of *Ruth Women Ministries* and *Chat&Chew Real Women Real Talk* Support Group. She has ministered the Love of Jesus Christ to countless women throughout the country.

Evangelist McKnight is married and has 6 children and 5 grandchildren. She Lives in Dallas, Texas.

Evangelist Cynthia McKnight

8431 Red Heart St
Arlington, Texas 76002
972-388-4050
Cynthiamcknight55@yahoo.com
FACEBOOK - Evangelist Cynthia McKnight
FACEBOOK - Chat&Chew Real Women
Real Talk
FACEBOOK - Mending Broken Hearts

Chapter 10
Just Close the Door

Minister Tonka Johnson

Recently I got a revelation while doing one of my devotions at home. I began to think how many of us saints are not as delivered as we think... Deliverance begins with you. In the book of **Luke 22:31**, Jesus explains to Peter that *"The Devil desires to Sift you as wheat"*

We have an adversary, the devil, who willingly uses our most vulnerable weaknesses against us. Find out where the enemy gains his knowledge about you.

When you have sinned in former nature in the flesh, the adversary becomes familiar with you. He knows your every move. If we watch Judas, before the last supper, Judas obtains the same power as the rest of the disciples. He saw blinded eyes opened, the dead raised, he saw Jesus calming the storm and walking on water. What prompted him to not stay in his current condition? What was his kryptonite? Greed and deception. The Bible says *"Therefore to him that knoweth to do good, and doeth it not, to him it is sin"* **(James 4:17) KJV**

Judas saw what was good and did it not. Deception will blind you. Sin will cause tunnel vision. Know that demonic strongholds work these areas. Demonic strongholds can be buried or hidden in a simple disguise.

The battlefield is the mind. The Mind is a warzone where Satan builds an entire arsenal around old thoughts from your past, from your feelings, emotions from the old relationships and old wounds. Within that, he uses this information for keeping you from moving into your real destiny and divine purpose.

Wounds of Rejection, pain, hurt, and bitterness can cause a spiritual cancer that will eat the foundation of revelation in any person. Anyone who is rejected can open a door to bitterness, and bitterness opens the door to revenge. Rejection is rooted in hate from someone else or pain that comes from their past or present relationships. Satan uses this as a weapon as well. This can open the door to sickness, disease or infirmity.

Bitterness can be rooted in rejection and if the person doesn't get full deliverance he or she will continue to be bound.

Know the Symptoms

We often deal with minor things in the body of Christ. Minor details like the outer appearance. The outer appearance is quite deceiving. You will be surprised how many people believe in legalism. Many people are dressed like supermodels and fashioned out of the latest magazines. Many are hurt and come to church with a smile, praise, and dance, and still are not delivered. We must be born again. **(John 3:7)**

Prayer & Fasting Are Major Keys

I learned to put prayer and fasting together. They are combustible elements in the spirit realm. We often chase after "Deep Revelation", but you cannot re-invent the wheel. You must pray. I think now more than ever prayer is very important. Deliverance and the closing of many doors in our lives cannot happen, until we turn our face and pray. Seek His face. Turn from our evil and perverse ways. Our land is sick because of lack of prayer and deliverance.

The Process

Confess the Lord as your personal savior. Ask for Forgiveness of any sins. Ask the Lord to save you and fill you with the Holy Spirit. Join a church that God has sent you to. If you are struggling in an area of deliverance, find someone who deals in the ministry in deliverance. Deliverance can take a process. Many want an overnight feeling, but in the book of **Mark 9:29,** *Jesus replied "these kind can come out through fasting and prayer."* If you are dealing with a particular stronghold, go on a fast; Let the enemy know that you are not playing around. Remember as I said earlier, that many don't realize the enemy knows our every move, especially when we are so predictable and have spent time with him through being unsaved or backslidden. Remember finding a church that believes in Deliverance is so important. Demons are real. They are not concerned about your religious traditions or your denominational attributes. Their assignment is to kill, steal, and destroy.

Territorial Spirits & Generation Curses

Under my leadership I've learned so much. One of the things that my leaders speak upon is Demonic Stronghold and territorial spirits. Demonic spirits can disappear for a season. In the Word of God, Jesus talks about the strongman coming into the house to spoil the goods, if we think that the enemy is vocal, think again. He is silent. Most snakes are silent and subtle. His ultimate job is squeezing the life out of you. We must be vocal and loud in our prayer time. Our adversary is the devil, who goes about like a roaring lion. He had access to heaven as well. In the book of **Job 1:7-8,** *God asked Satan a question, where are you going? He answered "I'm going to and fro, seeing whom I may devour."* Simply the enemy was giving God his declaration, his job, his assignment. The enemy's assignment was to destroy. When we deal with demons and territories we must understand that the enemy does what is allowed in that area. As saints we have the power to disallow what the enemy does in the earth realm. The enemy comes in through the open door that someone has left opened through sin. Sometimes this happens without us even knowing it. We leave doors open through sin, and once entry happens, it may be years before this same spirit resurfaces. Our adversary is a fugitive; he is a wanted man, but also a defeated foe. When we knowing or not knowingly sin, the doors are left open and if the enemy cannot destroy the ones that have a prayer life, he tries to destroy the ones that are out of the will of God. Remember the book of 1 Samuel; Saul was appointed by God, to become the 1st king of Israel. Anointed by Samuel the prophet, Saul was given the assignment to wipe out the Amaleks **(1Samuel 15:1-20).** When we look at how Saul lied to the prophet Samuel, concerning the destruction of the goods and treasures of the Amaleks, his behavior causes the spirit of the Lord to leave him.

The Bible says that an evil spirit came upon him that day forward. The disobedience of one man caused the door to be left open for an evil spirit to come upon him. Many don't realize that if you don't deal with your issues concerning yourself, they're doors that must be shut and demons know if you are serious or were just playing. They know because they're familiar spirits. Pray for your family. Intercede for your bloodline. Command the blessing of the Lord upon your family. Most of all pray for yourself.

Prayer to Release over the Bloodline

Father God,

I ask for forgiveness of any sin that I may have committed. Lord in the name of Jesus I plead the blood of Jesus around me and my family in the name of Jesus. I cancel every assignment in the name of Jesus over my family and over my generation. I break every generational curse off of my family and close every door that has been open knowingly and unknowingly in the name of Jesus. I let in the anointing of restoration, peace, joy, divine health, divine wealth, and divine power over my bloodline in the name of Jesus. You said that I'm the head and not the tail, above and not beneath, the lender and not the borrower. In Jesus' name we pray,

Amen.

MINISTER *Tonka Johnson* is a Native of St. Louis, Missouri. He grew up in church under the Late Rev. Elsa Hill and Bishop Dorothy Rhodes of St. Laura's Mission. In 2007, God Transplanted Minister Johnson in Springfield, Missouri. Minister Johnson is the current Intercessor at God's House of Glory in Springfield, Missouri, under the leadership of Pastors Henry & Chris Grandberry.

Minister Johnson works in the media & sound ministry. He began his training in ministry in 2010. Minister Johnson has currently founded his own business in 2015 called *Aknot Designs*. This service provides numerous services including Web Design, and Graphic flyers.

Minister Tonka Johnson

Springfield, MO 65804

AKNOTDESIGNS@YAHOO.COM

Conclusion

Forgiveness is For You

Prophetess Nell Dixon

What is Forgiveness? What does it mean to *Forgive* someone? What does real Forgiveness look like in a relationship? On my road to "Destiny Fulfilled" I have had the opportunity to experience what I called the Ultimate Forgiveness experience. Forgiving your family!!

Yes, I said it "FAMILY"!! For me when I think of family I think of loving support from people that know me best. I think of growing up in a community that not only supports my destiny but they also play a huge part in the success of me getting there. I think of growing up together, sharing memorable moments but most of all making lasting imprints in time that can never be erased…FAMILY!

What happens when the family as you knew it turns into your personal FOE? What happens to the family when life takes a dark turn down a path that leads to personal hurt and pain? Well, I found myself asking those same questions not long ago. Here is my personal journey of when I really lived out the echoes of what my heart had been saying during a very difficult period of my life "Forgiveness is *Really* for You".

When I was on this quest of getting to the root cause of all the friction, resentment, negative words and constant backstabbing that I was witnessing, it was at the hands of what I called family. My first HUMAN reaction was to purposely allow them to reap the exact same hurt that they were intentionally sowing toward me IMMEDIATELY!!! I couldn't wrap my mind around how they could be so intentional in sowing discord and negativity.

You see I was looking out the eyes of the victim and not the VICTOR! I couldn't understand how, now that my total disposition, attitude and outlook on life had changed for the better. Coming from a place of me immediately giving them the "SAME THING" and then some of what they were issuing out to me to its full extent and power.

However, those times and days were long gone and everyone in my family knew without a shadow of a doubt that my life had completely been given over to the Glory of God. Where was this level of disrespect coming from? I had to know. Where did the switch take place? I'm the same one that various family members would come to for prayer during difficult times in their lives. I would pray earnestly and

God would move on their behalf. I'm the same one that when something was going on in the family structure you could hear them echoing things like "did Nell dream anything", "have you told Nell what is going on" or "tell Nell and see what God is saying about this or that". Now all of a sudden, things had changed. Nevertheless, one thing I did know is that I was going to get to the root of this SPIRIT.

During my prayer time I would ask God to show me... "ME." Let's start there first! Let's take a deeper look on the inside that's reflecting my outward experience as it relates to others. I wanted to get the ROOT CAUSE OF THIS EFFECT, because the family dynamic had truly changed and it wasn't for the good. I looked to scripture where it says in **1 Peter 5:8 (KJV)**

[8] *Be sober, be vigilant; because your adversary the devil, as a roaring lion, walketh about, seeking whom he may devour:*

The moment I read that verse something in my spirit resonated with the scripture. Be sober, be vigilant because "your adversary the devil". The Bible clearly tells me that my adversary is the devil. The demonic influences that I was receiving at the hands of family were not my relative but the devil. I know the Word of God don't lie, can't lie and was my true answer to this situation. I began to take a deeper look at the root of this issue and I knew Forgiveness was the only answer to this situation. I had to forgive myself first and then forgive them whole heartily. Before I got to the place of forgiveness I really researched and prayed about what does TRUE FORGIVENESS look and feel like.

What are the steps to release people honestly out your heart and your experience? How do you still interact with those that have intentionally and maliciously mistreated you? What is Forgiveness?

Forgiveness is generally defined as a conscious, deliberate decision to release feelings of resentment or vengeance toward a person or group who has harmed you, regardless of whether they actually deserve your forgiveness. I am a firm believer that people will treat you the way "you" allow them.

Experts who study or teach forgiveness make it clear that when you forgive, you do not gloss over or deny the seriousness of an offense against you. Forgiveness does not mean forgetting, nor does it mean condoning or excusing offenses. Though forgiveness can help repair a damaged relationship, it doesn't obligate you to reconcile with the person or people who harmed you.

Instead, forgiveness brings the forgiver peace of mind and frees him or her from corrosive anger. Whether true forgiveness requires positive feelings toward the offender, experts agree that it at least involves letting go of deeply held negative feelings. In that way, it empowers you to recognize the pain you suffered without letting that pain define you, enabling you to heal and move on with your life.

Releasing negative feelings and emotions is vital to your overall Victory. Forgiveness is not so much for the ones that hurt you, but for YOU! What I have found out to be true is that on the road to "Destiny Fulfilled" there will be pot holes (unexpected circumstance). You may even encounter disappointment and some heartaches by those you thought would be there to celebrate your wins. Nevertheless, let me encourage you that whatever life brings you never give up on God. HE will never leave you nor forsake you! Let the light of God illuminate throughout your very being and shine forth in POWER.

Forgiveness is a powerful tool. Forgiveness frees you from the offense and the offender. Their tactics, negative words or intentional harm no longer hold you captive in the clutches of offense towards you. You take your power back when you release them. Freedom to live your life to the fullest for God's Glory is PRICELESS. Typically hurting people hurt other people. Let Forgiveness start with you. Even if your family doesn't understand your God-Given, predestined assignment over your life, don't let that stop you from fulfilling the God-Given Call on Your Life.

Remember *Forgiveness is For You*!

PROPHETESS *Nell Dixon* has been empowered with an immaculate three-fold Prophetic, Evangelistic, and Pastoral anointing to deliver the Word of God. Prophetess ministers with such boldness that causes even the hardest of hearts to be pierced by the love of God. Prophetess Nell Dixon is known as a woman after the heartbeat of God. This is very evident by the lifestyle of prayer, fasting, and holiness that she leads diligently before the Lord.

Prophetess Dixon has been commissioned to share the good news of Jesus Christ to the nations of the world. She is a devoted wife to Apostle C.D. Dixon, a mother of three beautiful children. Prophetess is an honor graduate of Hargest Business College graduating Magna Cum Laude in Accounting. With a social awareness of the economic issues of today's time, Prophetess Nell is also an entrepreneur.

Prophetess Dixon serves as a licensed and ordained Executive Pastor of Spiritual Temple World Headquarters where her husband,

Apostle C.D. Dixon, is both Senior Pastor and Overseer. Also, serving as the Executive Assistant to Apostle Dixon, Prophetess and Apostle Dixon are the proprietors of many conferences and events including but not limited to:

- *From Chains-2- Freedom*
- *The Refreshing Wind Prayer Clinic*
- *Prophetic Wind Radio Weekly Broadcast*
- *Get In The Flow Tour*
- *Couples with a Love Affair*
- *Empowering the Business Mind, Prophetic Youth Explosion*
- *Prophetic Night Live*
- *The Gift that Heals.*

Nell Dixon Ministries also hosted the "FIRE IN MY SOUL PRAYER CLINIC" October 23rd & 24th 2015 at the Lewisville Convention Center".

Prophetess Dixon is also a published author of a POWERFUL compilation book called *Get in the Flow ~ Destiny is Calling* and is one of the featured Co-authors of *Prayer Is the Master Key* compilation book with author Apostle C.D. Dixon and others scheduled to be released early 2016.

Envisioned with the mandate to point those that are lost **back** to JESUS, help the hurting, and empower those who really want change in their lives for the better, Prophetess Nell Dixon is fully equipped to take the message of Christ to the world.

Prophetess Nell Dixon

www.NellDixonMinistries.com
www.facebook.com/ProphetessNellDixon
www.twitter.com/ProphetessNellD
www.Instagram.com/ProphetessNellDixon
Periscope @ProphetessNellD

Email:
NellDixonMinistries@hotmail.com

Another Custom Compilation
Published by

ThrUs Publishing

"Birthing Books. Changing Lives."

ThrUs Publishing
Coppell Texas

www.ingramcontent.com/pod-product-compliance
Lightning Source LLC
Chambersburg PA
CBHW072023040426
42447CB00009B/1707